MACMILLAN BEGI

FIREFIGHTERS

To Georgie
With love from
Granma +
 Grandad
 xxx
25.6.90.

INTRODUCTION

This book is one of the *Macmillan Beginners* series. All these books talk about us or the world we live in. If there is a word you don't know, check in the Glossary at the back. There will probably be a picture to give you a clue. The pictures on every page of the book also give you clues about the words you are reading. Many of the things or people in the pictures have labels.

FIREFIGHTERS

Ron Thomas and Jan Stutchbury
Illustrated by Joanne Sisson

MACMILLAN BEGINNERS

Is that smoke?
Call the fire brigade!

At the fire station, in the control room, the telephone rings.

The alarm bell sounds!
Minutes later the firefighters
are on their way.

Stand back!
Big fire-engines speed down the street,
lights flashing, sirens screaming.

Traffic stops to let them through.
People stop to watch.

The firefighters work quickly
to put out the fire.

Long hoses are unrolled.
Huge ladders go up the side
of the building.

Firefighters climb ladders
to get closer to the fire.
They carry axes to smash the
windows to let the water in.

Hydraulic platform

Sometimes the firefighters are lifted up on a hydraulic platform, or 'H.P.' for short.

Oxygen cylinder

Inside the building
there is a lot of smoke.
Firefighters wear special
breathing apparatus.
It lets them breathe.

Somebody needs help! Up go the firefighters on the hydraulic platform to rescue them.

When the fire is out
the fire-engines go back to the station.
The fire-engines are washed
and the equipment is checked.

Firefighters are on call
all the time.
At night they stay at the fire station
in case they are needed.

Special clothes protect the firefighters from the fire.

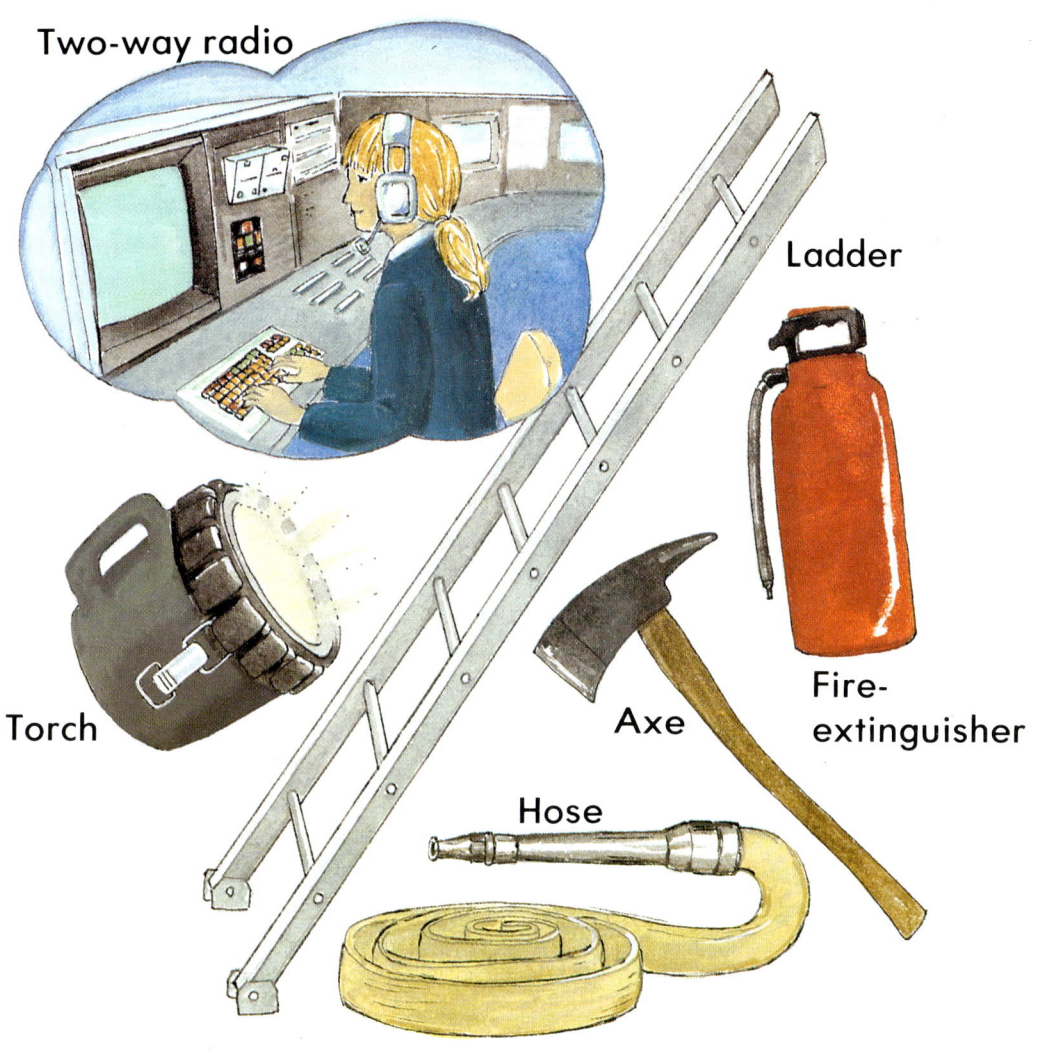

Special equipment helps them to do their job.

There is a training tower
at the fire station.
Firefighters practise climbing
ladders.

Water

Foam

Firefighters must know how to put out different kinds of fires. They use water or foam.

In the country, if there is
a forest fire, everybody fights it.

People from the farms and towns are the firefighters.

The radio in the fire shed tells the trucks where to go to fight the fire.

Sometimes a plane flies over the fire to drop water on the flames.

At school we have fire drill.
We practise leaving the building quickly and quietly.

Firefighters came to our school.
They brought their fire-engine.
They checked our fire-extinguishers.

Do you know the fire brigade's number?

Glossary

alarm bell	axes
building	extinguisher
fire station	fire-engine

© Ron Thomas and Jan Stutchbury 1988
Illustrations by Joanne Sisson

All rights reserved. No reproduction, copy or transmission of this publication may be made without written permission.

No paragraph of this publication may be reproduced, copied or transmitted save with written permission or in accordance with the provisions of the Copyright Act 1956 (as amended), or under the terms of any licence permitting limited copying issued by the Copyright Licensing Agency, 33–4 Alfred Place, London WC1E 7DP.

Any person who does any unauthorised act in relation to this publication may be liable to criminal prosecution and civil claims for damages.

First published in Great Britain 1988

Published by
MACMILLAN EDUCATION LTD
Houndmills, Basingstoke, Hampshire RG21 2XS
and London
Companies and representatives throughout the world

Published in Australia in 1987 by
The Macmillan Company of Australia Pty Ltd

Printed in Hong Kong

ISBN 0—333—47319—1